JOURNEY THROUGH OUR SOLAR SYSTEM

EXPLORING THE MOON

Published in 2018 by
KidHaven Publishing, an Imprint of Greenhaven Publishing, LLC
353 3rd Avenue
Suite 255
New York, NY 10010

Designer: Deanna Paternostro
Editor: Vanessa Oswald

Photo credits: Cover (background), back cover, p. 17 Vadim Sadovski/Shutterstock.com; cover (moon) Roobcio/Shutterstock.com; p. 5 godrick/Shutterstock.com; p. 7 paul prescott/Shutterstock.com; p. 9 Mopic/Shutterstock.com; p. 11 rangizzz/Shutterstock.com; pp. 12–13 HelenField/Shutterstock.com; p. 15 Procy/Shutterstock.com; p. 19 Patryk Kosmider/Shutterstock.com; p. 21 UniversalImagesGroup/Contributor/Universal Images Group/Getty Images.

Cataloging-in-Publication Data

Names: Alexander, Richard.
Title: Exploring the moon / Richard Alexander.
Description: New York : KidHaven Publishing, 2018. | Series: Journey through our solar system | Includes index.
Identifiers: ISBN 9781534522930 (pbk.) | 9781534522770 (library bound) | ISBN 9781534522497 (6 pack) | ISBN 9781534522671 (ebook)
Subjects: LCSH: Moon–Juvenile literature.
Classification: LCC QB582.A435 2018 | DDC 523.3–dc23
Printed in the United States of America

CPSIA compliance information: Batch #BS17KL: For further information contact Greenhaven Publishing LLC, New York, New York at 1-844-317-7404.

Please visit our website, www.greenhavenpublishing.com. For a free color catalog of all our high-quality books, call toll free 1-844-317-7404 or fax 1-844-317-7405.

CONTENTS

Moons of Planets 4

Our Moon 6

Earth's Ocean Tides 10

The Moon's Surface 12

Phases of the Moon 16

Astronauts on the Moon 20

Glossary 22

For More Information 23

Index 24

MOONS OF PLANETS

Moons look a lot like the planets in the **solar system**, but they're smaller in size. While planets **orbit** the sun, moons orbit the planets. Moons are also called natural **satellites**.

Earth's moon is the fifth-largest moon in the solar system.

OUR MOON

The moon we see in the night sky is Earth's only moon. Other planets' moons have names, but our moon is just called "the moon." Earth is about four times wider than the moon.

The moon is much smaller than Earth!

Plants, animals, and people don't live on the moon because there's very little air. The sky looks black from the moon because unlike Earth, it has a weak **atmosphere**.

Someone who weighs 100 pounds (45 kg) on Earth would weigh 16.6 pounds (7.5 kg) on the moon because it has less **gravity**.

EARTH'S OCEAN TIDES

The rise and fall of water **levels** in the ocean is called a tide. Tides are created by the pull of the moon's gravity.

The moon doesn't just look nice over the ocean. It plays a part in how the ocean moves.

THE MOON'S SURFACE

The surface of the moon is made up of rocks and dust.

There are highlands and lowlands on the moon. The highlands look white, and the lowlands look dark.

Astronauts have brought rocks from the moon back to Earth.

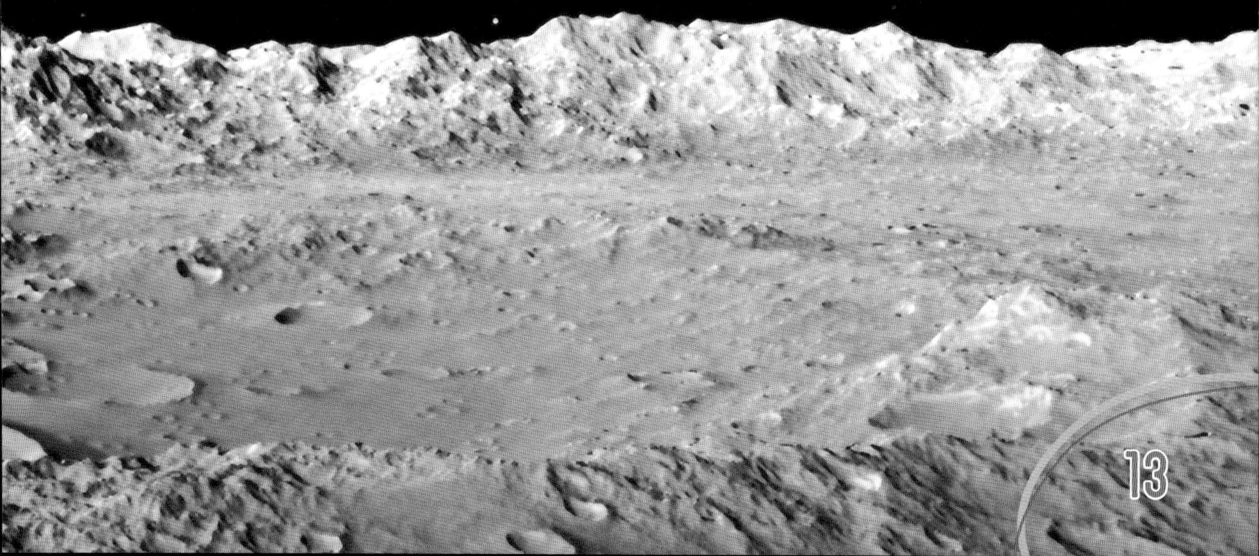

There are many craters on the moon. They look like holes of different sizes. These were made after space rocks hit the moon's surface many years ago.

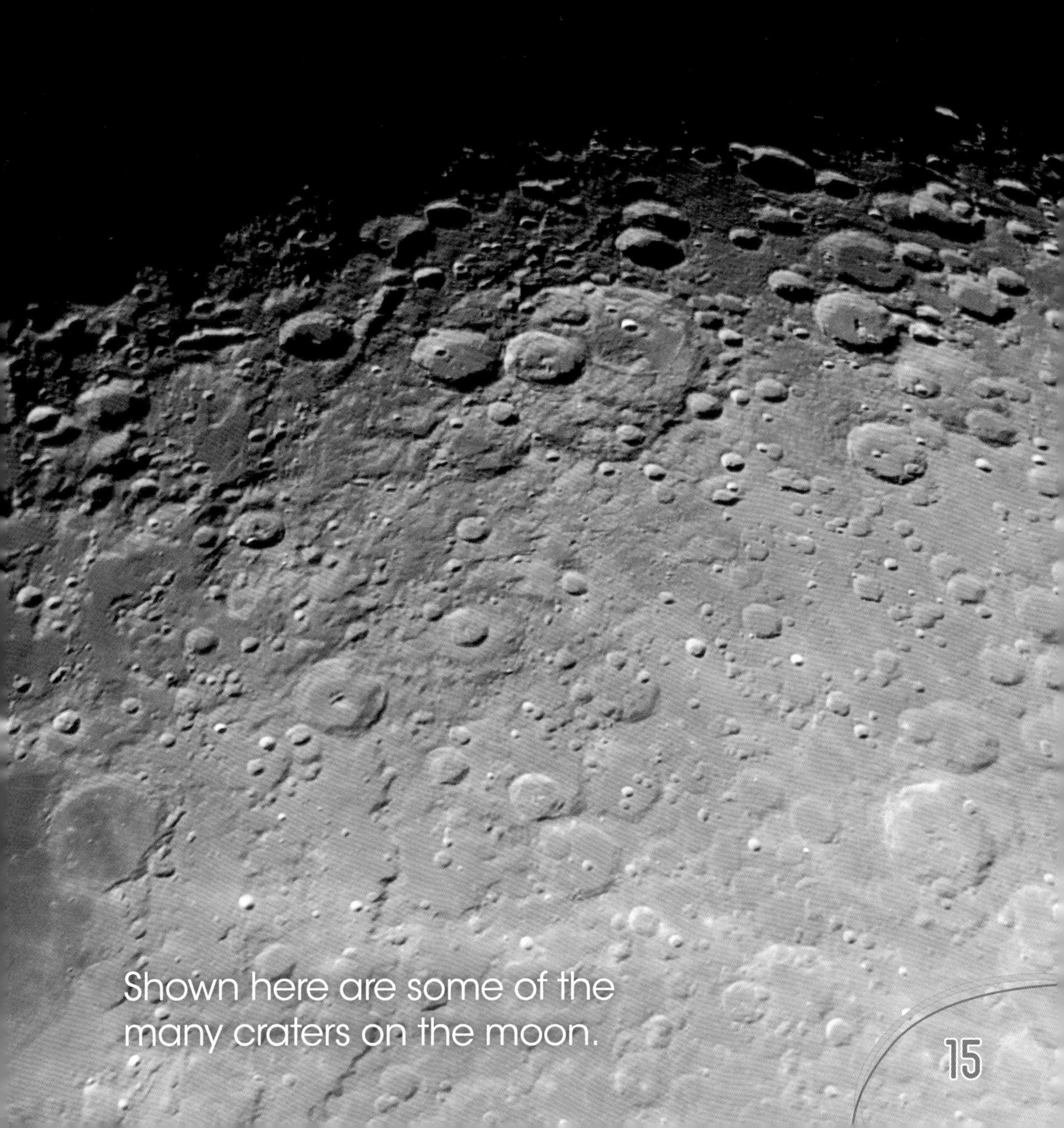

Shown here are some of the many craters on the moon.

PHASES OF THE MOON

Sunlight shines off of the moon, which is how we can see the moon in the night sky. The moon can't make its own light.

The sun is about 400 times farther away from Earth than the moon. However, they appear to look the same size in the sky because the sun is much bigger.

The moon goes through **phases** each month. During the moon's phases, it seems to change shape because of how much it's lit up by the sun at certain times.

The moon seems to have different shapes, shown here, as it orbits Earth.

ASTRONAUTS ON THE MOON

American astronauts first landed on the moon in 1969. Some scientists think that people may one day be able to live on the moon!

The law says no person or nation can own the moon.

GLOSSARY

astronaut: Someone who works in space.

atmosphere: Gases that make up the air around a planet.

gravity: The force that pulls objects toward the center of a planet, moon, or star.

level: Height or amount.

orbit: To travel in a circle or oval around something.

phase: A state in a set pattern of changes.

satellite: An object that moves around a much larger planet.

solar system: The sun and all the space objects that orbit it, including planets and their moons.

FOR MORE INFORMATION

Websites

NASA: Earth's Moon

solarsystem.nasa.gov/planets/moon/indepth
NASA's website features useful information about and photographs of the moon.

National Geographic Kids: Mission to the Moon

kids.nationalgeographic.com/explore/space/mission-to-the-moon/#moon-surface.jpg
This website provides cool moon facts and pictures of the moon.

Books

Harman, Alice. *Moon*. New York, NY: Windmill Books, 2016.

Taylor-Butler, Christine. *The Moon*. New York, NY: Children's Press, 2014.

Publisher's note to educators and parents: Our editors have carefully reviewed these websites to ensure that they are suitable for students. Many websites change frequently, however, and we cannot guarantee that a site's future contents will continue to meet our high standards of quality and educational value. Be advised that students should be closely supervised whenever they access the Internet.

INDEX

A
air, 8
astronaut, 13, 20

C
crater, 14, 15

D
dust, 12

E
Earth, 5, 6, 7, 8, 9, 10, 11, 19

G
gravity, 9, 10

H
highland, 13

L
light, 16
lowland, 13

N
natural satellite, 4

O
orbit, 4, 19

P
phase, 18, 19
planet, 4, 6

R
rocks, 12, 13, 14

S
solar system, 4, 5
space rock, 14
surface, 12, 14, 15

T
tide, 10